How Do Animals Use...
Their Wings?

Lynn Stone

Rourke
Publishing LLC
Vero Beach, Florida 32964

www.rourkepublishing.com

PHOTO CREDITS: All photos © Lynn Stone, excepts pg. 7, 13, 19 © Bruse Coleman

Editor: Robert Stengard-Olliges

Cover design by Michelle Moore.

Library of Congress Cataloging-in-Publication Data

Stone, Lynn M.
  How do animals use their wings? / Lynn Stone.
     p. cm. -- (How do animals use--?)
  ISBN-13: 978-1-60044-508-8
  1. Wings--Juvenile literature. I. Title.
  QL950.8.S76 2008
  591.47'9--dc22
                          2007016298

Printed in the USA

CG/CG

Rourke Publishing

www.rourkepublishing.com – rourke@rourkepublishing.com
Post Office Box 3328, Vero Beach, FL 32964

Many animals have wings.

Birds have wings.

Wings are very useful things.

Wings help some birds stay in one place.

Wings help some birds **fly** away.

Wings help some birds land.

And wings help some
birds swim.

If you had wings, how would you use them?

Glossary

bat (bat) – a small flying mammal

butterfly (BUHT uhr flie) – an insect with two pairs of wings

bird (burd) – an animal with wings

fly (flie) – to move through the air with wings

Index

Further Reading

Crawford, Tracy. *Birds*. Heinemann, 2006.
Perkins, Wendy. *Let's Look at Animal Teeth*. Pebble
  Press, 2007.

Websites

www.kidsites.com/sites-edu/animals.htm
animal.discovery.com

About the Author

Lynn M. Stone is the author of more than 400 children's books. He is a talented natural history photographer as well. Lynn, a former teacher, travels worldwide to photograph wildlife in its natural habitat.

WITHDRAWN